About the Author

Louisa Mastromarino, M.S.Ed, is a certified counselor educator. She holds a Bachelor of Arts Degree in Communications, a Master of Science Degree in School Counseling, and a post Masters' Degree in Supervision and Educational Leadership. She specializes in writing children books and in creating contemporary artworks. Her writings and artwork can be found at www.intuitivegalleries.com.

Spifford Max and the Cycle Pups
Go to Washington, D.C.

Louisa Mastromarino

Spifford Max and the Cycle Pups Go to Washington, D.C.

Olympia Publishers
London

www.olympiapublishers.com
OLYMPIA PAPERBACK EDITION

A CIP catalogue record for this title is available from the British Library.

ISBN: 978-1-78830-420-7

First Published in 2020

Olympia Publishers
Tallis House
2 Tallis Street
London
EC4Y 0AB

Printed in Great Britain

Dedication

This wonderful children's book, first in the Spifford Max series, is dedicated to my parents Lucille Mastromarino and Anthony Mastromarino in heaven.

Disclaimer

Children should always ride their bikes or vehicles outside with proper gear and with adult supervision.

Acknowledgments

I gratefully want to thank James Houghton, Jack Molton, Kristina Smith and Olympia Publishers for Spifford Max and the Cycle Pups Go to Washington D.C. I want to thank Stephanie Perna Slevin, Diane Zagaria Rice and Barbara Savin for their support. I also want to acknowledge Principal Kelly Speiser and the staff of Saint John's Lutheran School in Staten Island, New York for their diligence in teaching students history, reading, and writing.

To children everywhere: May history shine and may God be observed in all things.

My name is Spifford Max and I am the leader of the cycle pups! We love to ride our max cycle bikes throughout famous cities and towns. Today my cycle pup friends: Cycle Peter, Cycle Lucy, Cycle Stevie, and Cycle Mary and I are riding our cool max cycle bikes to the great American capital city of Washington, D.C. Washington, D.C. is where the United States President lives and works. Washington, D.C. is also the place where American laws are created and passed.

Today we will journey on our amazing max cycle bikes. They can do anything. They jump upstairs, move down rivers, make lots of fancy circles. Fill them up with soda pop and they roar with love. "Vroom, vroom!"

My cycle pup friends asked me to lead the way. Hooray! Washington, D.C. is my favorite place in the whole world and is named after America's first president, George Washington, who served as leader from 1789 to 1797.

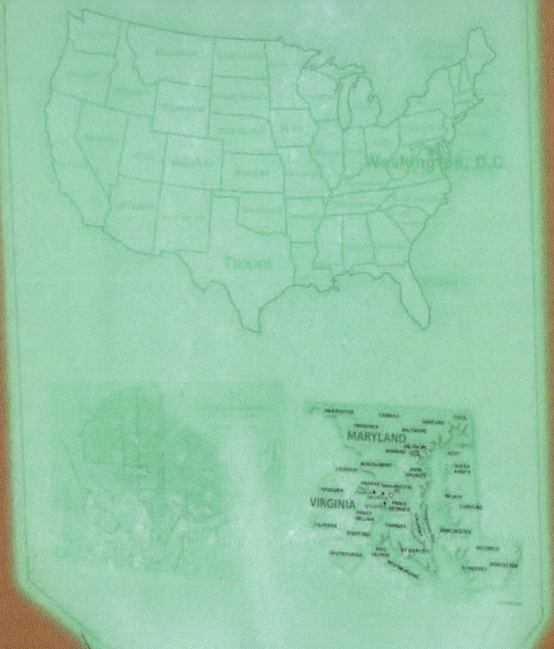

"Do you know where Washington, D.C. is, boys and girls? Spifford, use your laser projection watch to show us a picture," said Cycle Mary.

"Washington, D.C. is located in the District of Columbia," said Spifford Max. "That is what the 'D.C.' stands for. The District of Columbia is in the state of Maryland. Can you find the state of Maryland on your school map?"

"I love Washington, D.C." said Cycle Peter. "It has cherry trees that blossom in the spring and great historical landmarks and memorials."

"Today we are cycling up the majestic Potomac River… Whoosh…!" Said Spifford Max.

The grand Potomac River is located along the mid-Atlantic coast. Journey with us as we visit four of the most famous landmarks in the world: the Capitol Building, where Congress meets, the Lincoln and Jefferson Memorial, in honor of America's former presidents, and the illustrious White House, where the current president and his family reside.

VROOM

VROOM

"Hey everyone, vroom vroom, and up we go along the river to the Capitol Building built from 1793 to 1829. Come on, everyone, we can ride up the Capitol Steps," said Spifford.

The Capitol Building has a white dome on top and the design of the landmark was inspired by Greek and Roman architecture.

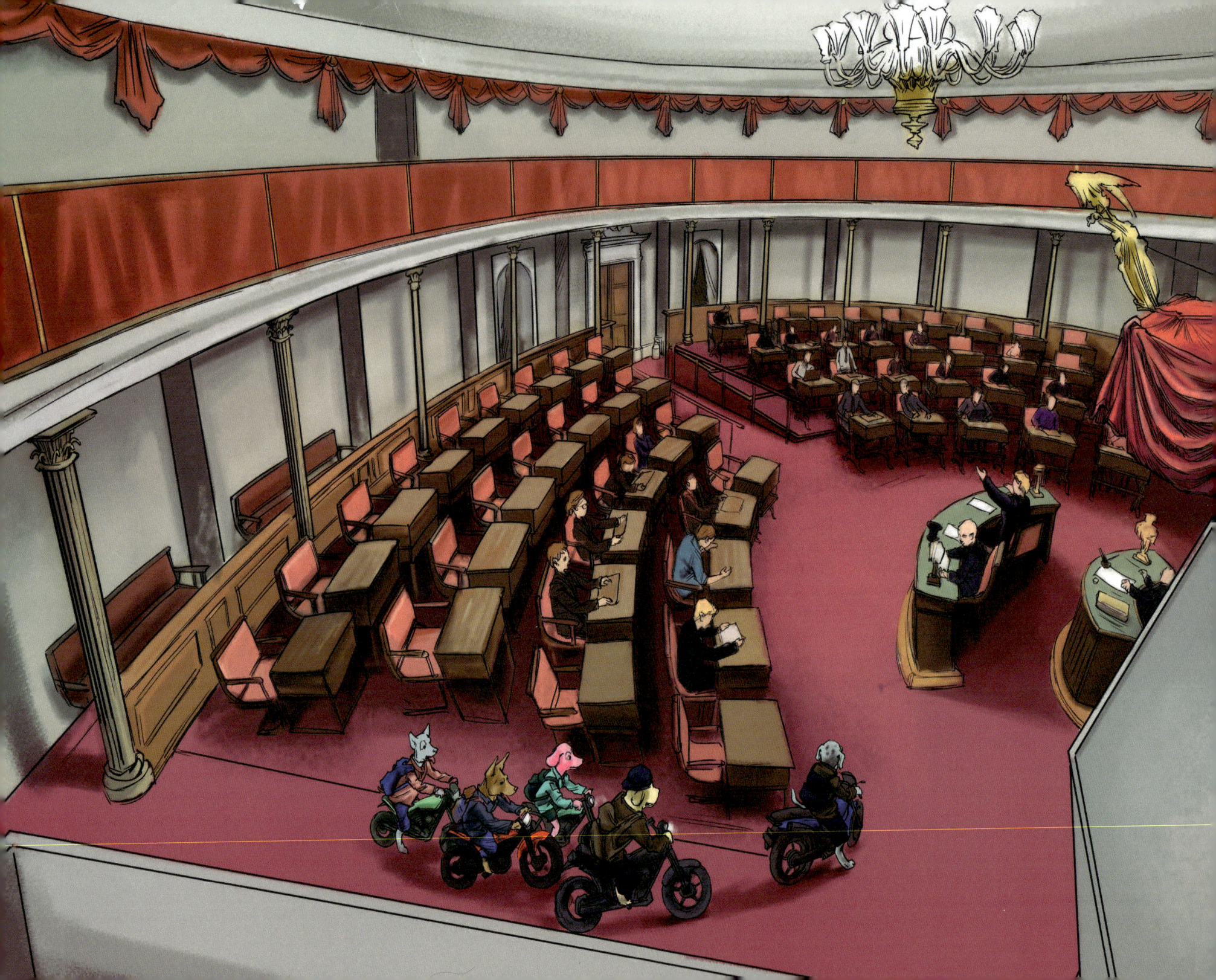

America has three branches of government: the executive branch, the legislative branch and the judicial branch. The House of Representatives and the Senate, the legislative branch, reside in the Capitol Building. The House and the Senate are responsible for creating laws.

"Wow, Spifford, I can't wait to be a senator one day," said Cycle Stevie.

"Me too," said Cycle Lucy. "We will get to write bills and create a better world."

"Zoom, zoom… whoosh," said Cycle Peter. "Hey, let's all ride fast away to the Lincoln Memorial, the grandest site to see."

The Lincoln Memorial celebrates Abraham Lincoln, the sixteenth president of the United States and his accomplishments. The majestic Lincoln Memorial stands 134 feet wide and 99 feet tall.

"It is massive," said Spifford Max.

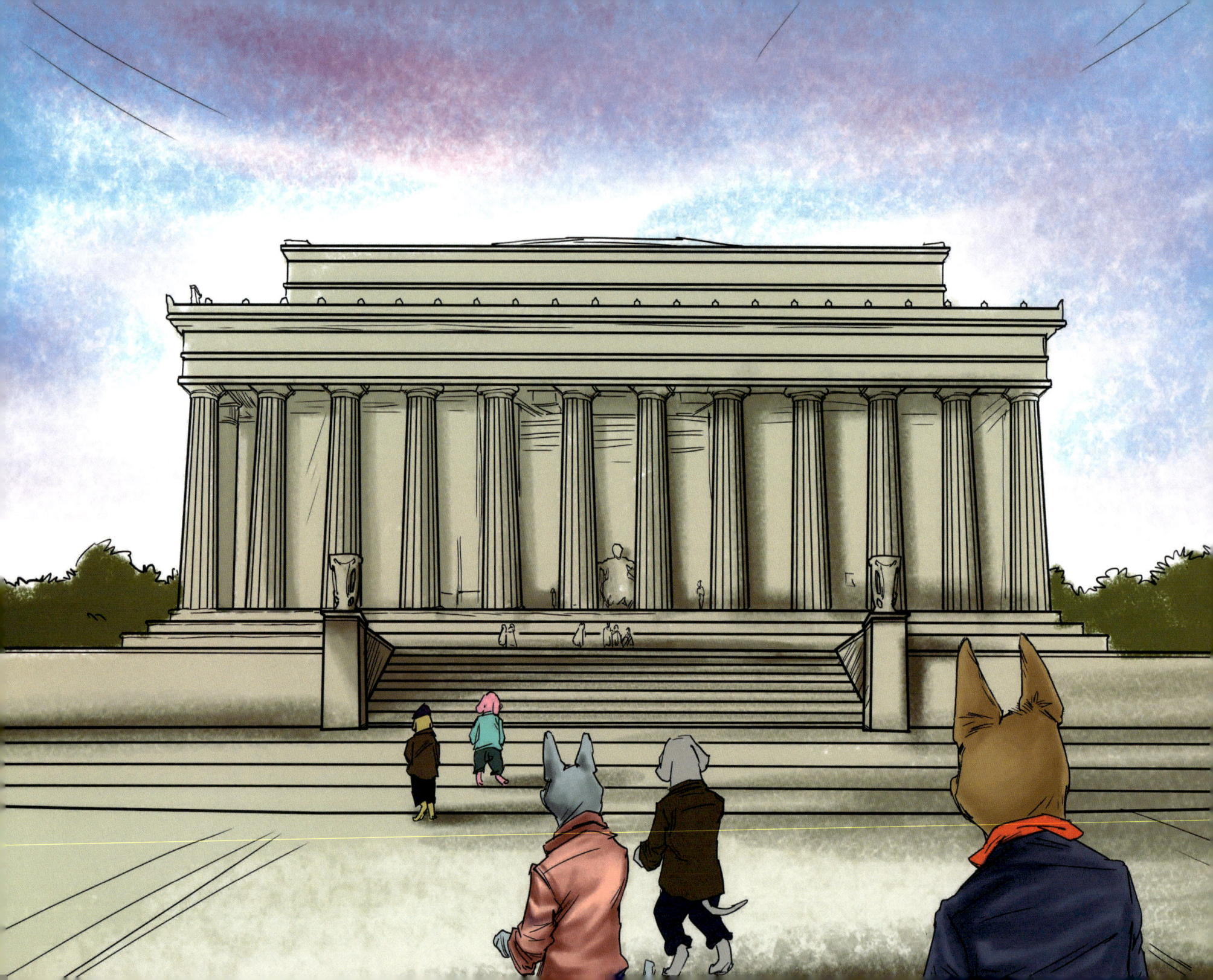

I love Abraham Lincoln. He wrote the Emancipation Proclamation and used negotiation skills to end the Civil War in order to abolish slavery. There is an inscription carved on the back of the Lincoln Memorial that celebrates liberty.

"The inscription reads 'In this temple, as in the hearts of the people for whom he saved the Union, the memory of Abraham Lincoln is enshrined forever'," said Cycle Mary.

"How Amazing!" Said Cycle Stevie.

After riding to the memorial's edge, all of the Cycle Pup friends looked on at the great statue with a smile and a freedom song.

Let's get on board the steam tugboat and ride along the majestic Potomac River to the Jefferson Memorial, completed in 1943 to honor Thomas Jefferson, the third president of the United States. He is one of American history's most revered presidents.

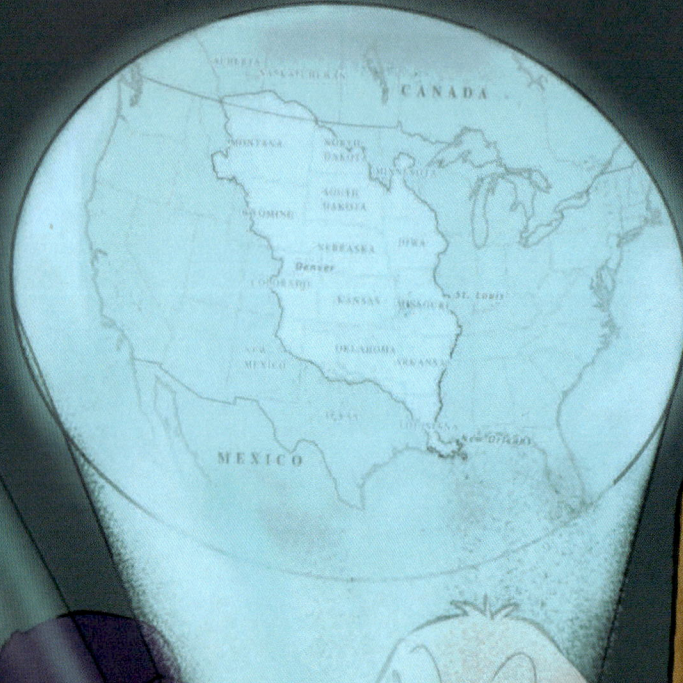

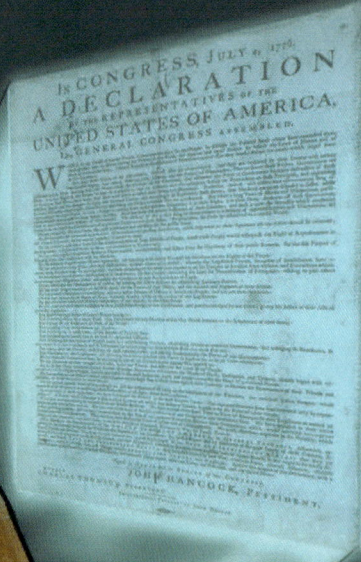

"Wow! Hey look at this laser projection about Thomas Jefferson. Thomas Jefferson authored the Declaration of Independence, the document that founded America, sponsored the expedition of Lewis and Clark, two famous explorers, and purchased the Louisiana Territory from the French leader Napoleon Bonaparte in 1803," said Cycle Peter.

"Thomas Jefferson was a musician and a very kind-hearted person too," said Cycle Lucy. "I want to be just like him."

"Me too, vroom zoom," said Cycle Mary. "For me the Jefferson Memorial stands as a reminder to the American nation that freedom still rings."

"Now let's race to the amazing White House to meet up with the President and his staff. The White House was built from 1792 to 1800 and has 132 rooms. It has 600,000 visitors per year and is one of the most 'happenin'' places on earth," said Spifford Max.

"Whee," said Cycle Peter, "Let's ride through some of the famous rooms."

"O boys and girls, here we go!" said everyone.

"The room I love the best is the Oval Office," said Spifford. "The Oval Office is where the President and his staff including the Vice President and his Secretary of State meet to solve the world's problems."

"I love this room too," said Cycle Stevie.

"Whee…! We can ride around and see all the historical artifacts," said Cycle Lucy.

"Hey, look at that the full-length portrait of George Washington by Gilbert Stuart! It is grand!" said Cycle Peter. "I want to take a picture of myself in front of it."

"Let's all take a picture!" said Spifford Max.

Spifford Max and the Cycle Pups stopped to take a picture with the immortal Washington.

"Now let's ride to the master Lincoln Bedroom," said everyone.
The Lincoln bedroom is the favorite room of most of the home's guests.
That is the room where the president himself, Abe Lincoln, used as his office.

"The bed was made of rosewood and purchased by his wife, Mrs. Mary Todd Lincoln, for formal guest visits," said Cycle Mary.

"Wow!" said Cycle Peter.

"Mr. Lincoln worked long hours in the Lincoln bedroom. He fought for freedom and signed the Emancipation Proclamation in this room," said Spifford Max.

"Hey Spifford," said Cycle Stevie. "Let's ride away to the busiest room in the house, the Cabinet Room."

"The President and his cabinet members meet in the Cabinet Room to make decisions about the economy and world peace. Wow! I love the way everyone works together to have fun! I love the way everyone's goal is to create lasting freedom!" said Spifford Max.

"Hey all," said the group. "We are done for today. Let's race out the door 'vroom vroom' and on our way back to the grand Potomac River."

Spifford Max and the Cycle Pups headed back home. They love to ride their max cycle bikes to famous places all the time. You will see them ride away in the sun, having fun, sipping soda, and loving history in motion.

"Have a great day," the Cycle Pups say. "And see you soon in your favorite place! Hooray!"

CYCLE PUPS SUGGESTED WRITING AND DISCUSSION ACTIVITIES AFTER THE READING

1. Have the students write about a famous city that they visited or plan to visit. Discuss their favorite landmark.

2. Have students draw a picture of the Capitol Building, the Lincoln Memorial, the Jefferson Memorial or the White House and post the pictures on the class bulletin board.

3. Have students use the internet to research historical facts about Washington, D.C. and present them to the class.

4. Have students research one president of the United States mentioned in the story. Celebrate the presidents in preparation for Presidents' Day, the third Monday in February.

"I love the White House and can't wait to be president too one day," said Cycle Lucy. "I can't wait to change the world for the better and be a great leader."

"You will be a wonderful leader," said Spifford Max, "and so would everyone reading this book!"

5. Have students research historical documents such as the Declaration of Independence and the Emancipation Proclamation and present their findings.

6. Where should Spifford Max and the Cycle Pups travel next? Write a short story about their adventures in the place that you choose.

7. Research vocabulary terms: negotiation, emancipation, memorial, economy, architecture, etc. Have fun learning new words and adding them to your stories and projects.

CPSIA information can be obtained at www.ICGtesting.com
Printed in the USA
BVIW120149170720
583608BV00005BA/191